Wonders
of the World

Wonders
of the World

Brian Williams

Miles Kelly
PUBLISHING

Author
Brian Williams

Designed, Edited and Project Managed by
Starry Dog Books

Editor
Belinda Gallagher

Assistant Editor
Mark Darling

Artwork Commissioning
Lesley Cartlidge

Indexer
Janet De Saulles

Art Director
Clare Sleven

Editorial Director
Paula Borton

First published in 2001 by
Miles Kelly Publishing Ltd
The Bardfield Centre
Great Bardfield
Essex CM7 4SL

24681097531

Some material in this book can also be found in *The Greatest Book of the Biggest and Best*

A British Library Cataloguing-in-Publication Data.
A catalogue record for this book is available from the British Library

ISBN 1-84236-066-3

Printed in China

www.mileskelly.net
info@mileskelly.net

CONTENTS

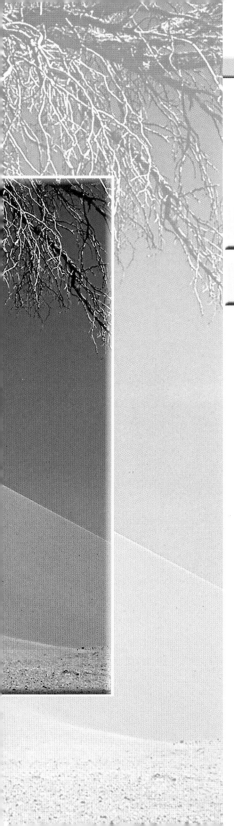

WONDERS OF
THE WORLD

The world is filled with amazing sights both natural and man made. The beautiful wildlife havens of Tanzania in Africa are home to many protected animals, while in North America the course of the Colorado River continues to carve its way through the Grand Canyon, the world's biggest gorge.

For centuries man has built great monuments. Some have become lost wonders of ancient times, like the mighty Colossus of Rhodes, a huge bronze statue which towered 37 m high. Some remain, like the puzzling pyramids of Egypt, enormous four-sided structures built as tombs for ancient Egyptian kings. Even today huge structures of incredible height and size are built, like the amazing stainless steel Gateway to the West in the USA. It stands at an incredible 192 m high, and visitors can take a tram to the top.

Explore the biggest and best facts of the *Wonders of the World* and discover some monumental sights. There are the big, serious facts – for reference – and less serious ones, too, for fun. These pages are packed with some of the biggest and best, oddest and strangest, smallest and funniest facts around!

◀ THE NAMIB DESERT, AFRICA

AWESOME PLACES

Climate, wind and water have created and shaped Earth's natural wonders, many of which have existed for millions of years. They have been on Earth far longer than human beings and will still be here in millions of years time. The Great Rift Valley in East Africa, for example, is a 3,000-km-long gash across Earth's surface, containing many great lakes and huge volcanic craters such as Ngorongoro in Tanzania. Shorter than the Rift Valley, but mightily impressive, is the Grand Canyon in the USA. It is the largest gorge in the world, and is being cut from the rock by the Colorado River. Such awesome places fill us with wonder.

▲ The Aboriginal name for Ayers Rock in central Australia is Uluru, which means 'great pebble'! The world's biggest 'pebble' is a lump of sandstone standing 348 m high, more than 2.4 km long and 1.6 km wide. It is more than 480 million years old.

◀ The Karakorum range on the border of Pakistan and China has some of the world's highest mountains, including the second-highest peak, K2, which towers 8,611 m above sea level. On mountains this high, the snow never melts.

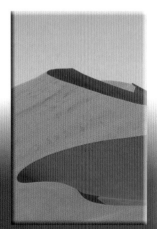

◀ The Namib Desert in southwest Africa is the world's oldest desert. It covers more than 270,000 sq km. Parts of this desolate region have less than 2 cm of rainfall a year. Sand dunes in the Namib Desert can be up to 244 m high.

▶ Monument Valley in the American state of Utah (shown here and below) has a stark and beautiful landscape, much loved by the makers of Western films. Towers of red sandstone rock, carved by wind and water, rise from the valley floor.

» Strangest rock formation: Giant's Causeway, Ireland   » Biggest rock arch: Landscape Arch, Utah, USA

▲ One of the most amazing natural wildlife reserves in the world is Tanzania's Ngorongoro Crater, an extinct volcanic crater in the Great Rift Valley of Africa. Within a huge natural bowl live thousands of birds like these flamingoes, along with herds of antelope, zebra and wildebeest.

DID YOU KNOW?
The rocks of the Grand Canyon in Colorado, USA, appear vividly coloured at sunset, attracting thousands of tourists. The canyon measures 446 km long, 1.5 to 29 km wide and about 1.6 km at its deepest point. The oldest and deepest rocks in the canyon are from 1.7 to 2 billion years old, and have been worn away by the action of the Colorado River.

▶ The Giant's Causeway is a natural wonder in Northern Ireland. About 40,000 hexagonal pillars of volcanic basalt rock stand by the sea. Legend tells how the giant Finn MacCool piled up the stones to make a bridge to Scotland.

▲ In Petrified Forest National Park, Arizona, USA, visitors can sit on stone trees 225 million years old. The trees were buried by mud and ash, and over time the minerals hardened into stone, or 'petrified', forming stone tree trunks.

▶▶	FIVE COLOURFUL NATURAL WONDERS
White Sands, New Mexico, USA	Pure white gypsum sands
Laguna Colorado, Bolivia	Tomato-red, algae-filled lagoon
Mato Grosso, Brazil	Vast expanse of green rainforest
Painted Desert, Arizona, USA	Multicoloured sandstone landscape
Wave Rock, Western Australia	Yellow, 15-m high wave-shaped rock

PUZZLING PYRAMIDS

People of the ancient world built astonishing artificial mountain-temples and tombs as far apart as Africa and Mexico, using only their bare hands. Many of these huge structures are still standing. In Iran and Iraq, where they are called ziggurats, and in Mexico and Central America, the pyramids were crowned with temples. But the most famous pyramids were built in Egypt as tombs. For more than 4,000 years visitors have marvelled at the size and construction of these colossal monuments, and wondered how they were built so big, and why.

▲ *The three enormous, four-sided pyramids at Giza in Egypt were built as tombs for Egypt's kings about 4,500 years ago. They were the biggest, and are the only surviving, of the Seven Wonders of the ancient world.*

▼ *The Sphinx is a 73-m-long, 20-m-high stone creature that sits beside the Great Pyramid, the largest of the pyramids at Giza in Egypt. Some historians believe that its base, shaped like the body of a lion, is older than its head, which was added later. The head is thought to represent Khafre, son of the Pharaoh Khufu who reigned from 2900 to 2877 BC.*

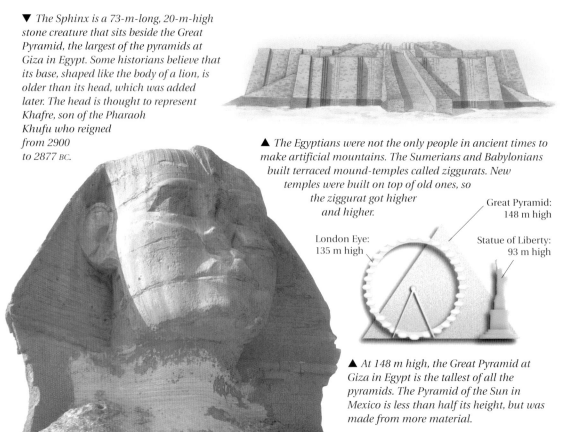

▲ *The Egyptians were not the only people in ancient times to make artificial mountains. The Sumerians and Babylonians built terraced mound-temples called ziggurats. New temples were built on top of old ones, so the ziggurat got higher and higher.*

London Eye:
135 m high

Great Pyramid:
148 m high

Statue of Liberty:
93 m high

▲ *At 148 m high, the Great Pyramid at Giza in Egypt is the tallest of all the pyramids. The Pyramid of the Sun in Mexico is less than half its height, but was made from more material.*

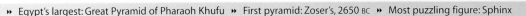

GIANTS

● The biggest pyramid in Mexico is bigger in volume than the Great Pyramid in Egypt.

● Pyramids in the Americas were made from vast piles of earth covered with stones. Temples were constructed on top.

● Egyptian pyramids were all stone. Tunnels inside led to burial chambers for kings and queens.

▲ *Without metal tools or the wheel, the Maya people of Mexico and Central America built great pyramids deep in the jungle, like this one at Chichén Itzá in Mexico. The pyramids were used for religious ceremonies, including human sacrifices.*

➤➤ GREAT PYRAMID FACTS	
Length of base on each side	230 m
Area of base	5 hectares (or 8 soccer pitches)
Number of stones	About 2.3 million
Average weight of each stone	2.5 tonnes
Weight of biggest stone	290 tonnes
Labour force and time taken	100,000 men, about 20 years

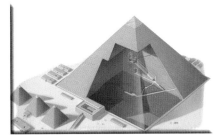

▲ *Inside the Great Pyramid of King Khufu were chambers full of treasure, reached by long passages. These were sealed after the king was buried to keep out robbers.*

▼ *Thousands of workers were used to construct the pyramids. All the work was done by human muscles, hauling the stones on rollers and sledges, and up ramps. The largest pyramid contains more than 2 million stones.*

LOST WONDERS OF THE ANCIENT WORLD

In the 100s BC a Greek writer named Antipater listed seven sights that no tourist in the Greek and Roman world should miss. These fabulous sights were the biggest and most amazing constructions of their time, and became known as the 'Seven Wonders of the World'. Today, only the pyramids of Egypt still stand. Little remains of the other six wonders. The shortest-lived was the Colossus of Rhodes, a giant statue about as high as the Statue of Liberty in New York. It stood for less than 20 years before being toppled by an earthquake.

▲ *Locations of the Seven Wonders of the ancient world: 1) Statue of Zeus, Greece. 2) Temple of Artemis, Turkey. 3) Colossus of Rhodes. 4) Mausoleum, Turkey. 5) Hanging Gardens, present-day Iraq. 6) Lighthouse at Alexandria, Egypt. 7) Pyramids, Egypt.*

▲ *At 12 m high, the statue of the Greek god Zeus at Olympia was six times human-size and was made of ivory and gold. People who came to the Olympic Games visited the god's temple to marvel at the statue inside.*

▶ *The Mausoleum, or tomb, of King Mausolus, built about 353 BC, was so impressive that from then on all large tombs were called 'mausoleums'. It was made of marble blocks.*

▶ *No remains have ever been found of the Hanging Gardens of Babylon, but historians think they were built somewhere near Baghdad, in Iraq, by King Nebuchadnezzar. The only surviving description of them was written by a priest some 400 years after they were built. The Gardens probably looked like a ziggurat (a brick-pyramid), covered with terraces of trees and plants.*

the Gardens were built for the king's sick wife, who missed her green mountain home

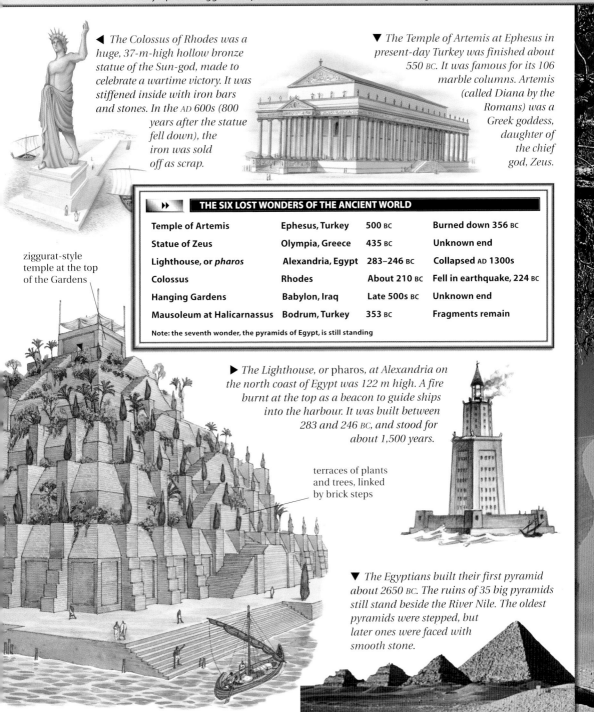

◀ *The Colossus of Rhodes was a huge, 37-m-high hollow bronze statue of the Sun-god, made to celebrate a wartime victory. It was stiffened inside with iron bars and stones. In the* AD *600s (800 years after the statue fell down), the iron was sold off as scrap.*

▼ *The Temple of Artemis at Ephesus in present-day Turkey was finished about 550* BC. *It was famous for its 106 marble columns. Artemis (called Diana by the Romans) was a Greek goddess, daughter of the chief god, Zeus.*

ziggurat-style temple at the top of the Gardens

▸▸ THE SIX LOST WONDERS OF THE ANCIENT WORLD

Temple of Artemis	**Ephesus, Turkey**	**500** BC	**Burned down 356** BC
Statue of Zeus	**Olympia, Greece**	**435** BC	**Unknown end**
Lighthouse, or *pharos*	**Alexandria, Egypt**	**283–246** BC	**Collapsed** AD **1300s**
Colossus	**Rhodes**	**About 210** BC	**Fell in earthquake, 224** BC
Hanging Gardens	**Babylon, Iraq**	**Late 500s** BC	**Unknown end**
Mausoleum at Halicarnassus	**Bodrum, Turkey**	**353** BC	**Fragments remain**

Note: the seventh wonder, the pyramids of Egypt, is still standing

▶ *The Lighthouse, or* pharos, *at Alexandria on the north coast of Egypt was 122 m high. A fire burnt at the top as a beacon to guide ships into the harbour. It was built between 283 and 246* BC, *and stood for about 1,500 years.*

terraces of plants and trees, linked by brick steps

▼ *The Egyptians built their first pyramid about 2650* BC. *The ruins of 35 big pyramids still stand beside the River Nile. The oldest pyramids were stepped, but later ones were faced with smooth stone.*

MOUNDS, STONES AND CIRCLES

Why did ancient peoples spend so much time and energy building circles of stones and wood, and piling up mounds of earth? Historians believe that some of the stone circles, such as the world-famous Stonehenge in England, were used for religious ceremonies. Standing stones and mounds, or barrows, from the early metalworking period, were often put up on top of high hills, and generally marked the burial site of a powerful person. But the purpose of some prehistoric sites remains a mystery. Some 1,500 years ago in Peru, the Nazca people scraped giant soil-pictures of creatures so big that they can only be seen properly from the air.

▲ *At Carnac in northwest France, more than 3,000 granite 'standing stones' make up the biggest group of prehistoric stones in the world. Some are single stones, others are in groups or long lines.*

▼ *The people of Stone Age Britain constructed Stonehenge, an extraordinary and unique sacred site, over a period of about 1,400 years (2950 to 1600 BC). It started as a ring of ditches, and later giant stones, some from as far as 380 km away, were put up. The biggest upright stones are 9 m long and weigh 50 tonnes. Stonehenge may have been a temple, a meeting place or an astronomical observatory.*

» Biggest prehistoric mound in Europe: Silbury Hill, UK » Strangest drawings: Nazca lines, Nazca Desert, Peru

» FAMOUS PREHISTORIC CIRCLES AND MOUNDS		
Stonehenge, England	Rings of cut stones	Between 2950 and 1600 BC
Silbury Hill, England	Burial mound 40 m high	About 3000 BC
Carnac, France	3,000 standing stones	Dates vary, about 2000 BC
Avebury, England	Stone circles and earth banks	About 2000 BC

▼ Easter Island in the South Pacific is famous for its 600 mysterious stone faces. The tallest are 12 m high. They were put up more than 1,000 years ago by the original Polynesian settlers. No-one knows why!

◄ Silbury Hill in southern England (not far from Stonehenge) is the biggest mound made by prehistoric people in Europe. Over 3,000 years old, the chalk mound is 40 m high and covers an area as big as 3 soccer pitches. In 1970 a burial mound or barrow was discovered inside.

▶ What looks like a giant snake coiled in the woodland of Ohio, USA, is actually an earth mound. Called the Great Serpent Mound, it was made more than 2,000 years ago. There are hundreds of similar mounds across North America.

▼ In the Nazca Desert of Peru, ground art exists on a huge scale, its purpose a mystery. There are geometric patterns and drawings of fish, birds such as this humming bird, spiders and a monkey. They are visible properly only from the air, but were created long before any known form of air travel!

TEMPLES AND TOMBS

The stories surrounding temples and tombs excite the imagination – a lost temple in the jungle, a Greek temple high on a hill, an underground tomb filled with clay soldiers, a marble tomb for an emperor's wife. The ancient Egyptians were the greatest temple and tomb-builders, matched only by the Chinese, who buried an army of terracotta soldiers to guard the emperor Shih Huangdi in the afterlife. This 2,000-year-old tomb was unearthed in 1979. A century before, in the 1860s, a French explorer in Cambodia glimpsed stone towers among the jungle trees. He had rediscovered the enormous Hindu temple of Angkor Wat.

▲ *Kings of Egypt were buried in rock tombs in the Valley of the Kings, near the city of Luxor. So far 62 tombs have been found there, the largest being that of King Seti.*

▼ *The incredible temple-city of Angkor Wat in Cambodia was built between 1113 and 1150 for King Suryavarman II, ruler of the Khmer Empire. It is the largest complex of religious buildings in the world, and includes this Hindu temple with its 70-m-high towers. Some 80,000 people lived in Angkor Wat, until it was abandoned about 1440.*

▲ *Probably the most famous of all Greek temples is the Parthenon in Athens. It was built on the Acropolis Hill between 447 and 432 BC to honour the city's patron-goddess, Athena. In 1687 it was badly damaged by a gunpowder explosion.*

▲ *The Taj Mahal was built for Mumtaz Mahal, wife of the Mogul emperor of India, Shah Jahan. When she died in 1629, her husband ordered the most beautiful tomb in the world to be built for her. It took 20,000 people 20 years to complete. The emperor and his wife are buried together under the 60-m-high, white marble dome.*

IT'S A FACT
The biggest temple ever built was the Temple of Amun at Karnak in Egypt (about 1250 BC). Its courts and pillared halls were bigger than Angkor Wat, but hardly anyone walked through them. Only priests were allowed inside the enormous sacred building.

▼ *The terraced temple of Borobudur in Java, Indonesia, is the biggest Buddhist temple in the world, with pinnacles over 30 m high. Started in the 700s, its three-sphere plan represents the three stages of human life – passion, visible world and spiritual world.*

▸▸ BIGGEST TEMPLES	
NAME	**DATE**
1 ★ Temple of Amun, Egypt	About 1250 BC
2 Temple of Angkor Wat, Cambodia	AD 1113–1150
3 Temple of Borobudur, Indonesia	AD 778–850

▶ *The awesome rock temples at Petra in Jordan were built in the 1st and 2nd centuries AD, when Petra was a rich trading city under Roman rule. It is known as the 'rose-red city' after the colour of the rock. Petra declined after AD 350, but its Street of Façades, which includes the famous treasury of Khazneh, shown here, is well preserved.*

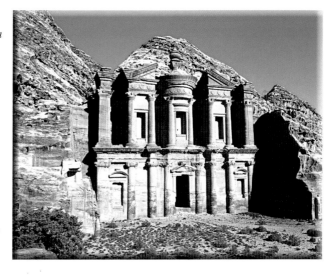

» Biggest church: in Ivory Coast » Tallest cathedral spire: Ulm's, Germany » Oldest stained glass: in Germany, 1050

CHURCHES AND MOSQUES

Some of the world's biggest and most beautiful and inspiring buildings are churches and mosques. Sometimes one mighty building has served two faiths. The great Christian church of Hagia Sophia, for example, built in Constantinople (modern Istanbul), later became a Muslim mosque. Cathedral builders built towers and spires that rose towards the heavens, but sometimes they aimed too high – the main spire of Lincoln Cathedral was the highest in the world (160 m) until 1548, when it collapsed. The world's biggest church is the Basilica in the Ivory Coast, Africa.

▲ *The world's biggest cathedral (though not the biggest church) is the Cathedral of St John the Divine in New York City. Construction of this medieval-style church began in 1892, but was interrupted between 1941 and 1979. The nave is 183 m long.*

▼ *St Peter's Basilica in the Vatican City is the largest Christian church in Europe. It is 218 m long and covers 23,000 sq m (four soccer pitches). St Peter's was built between 1506 and 1614. Many great Renaissance artists contributed to the project, which was designed to amaze the Christian world.*

The huge dome of St Peter's measures 42 m across. Visitors can climb up inside it to the gallery at the top.

from this balcony the Pope blesses pilgrims at the great festivals of Christmas and Easter

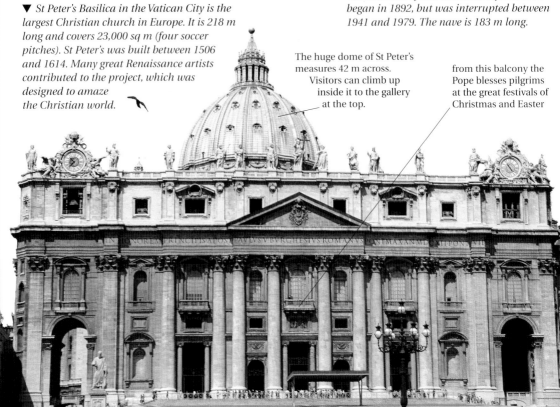

▼ *The Great Hassan II Mosque in Casablanca, Morocco, has the tallest minaret or tower of any Islamic mosque. It is 200 m high. The mosque was completed in 1993. The faithful are called to prayer five times a day by calls that are broadcast from the minaret. When they hear the call to prayer, Muslims generally stop what they are doing and either go into a prayer room, or put down a prayer mat wherever they are, and pray.*

▲ *The world's biggest mosque is the Shah Faisal Mosque on the outskirts of Pakistan's capital city, Islamabad, which means 'place of Islam'. The mosque has space for 300,000 worshippers in its main prayer hall, which is shaped like a giant desert tent, and in its grounds.*

◀ *There are higher crosses on modern church masts, but the tallest cathedral spire, at 161 m high, is that of Ulm Cathedral in Germany. The cathedral was begun in 1377, but the immense stone tower at its western end was not finished until 1890.*

▼ *In Djenne in central Mali, the Great Mosque – made mostly of sun-dried mud – has been a place of religious worship since the 1300s. About this time, the religion of Islam reached this part of north Africa, and Mali became a centre of Islamic scholarship.*

▸▸ FAMOUS BRITISH CATHEDRALS

St Paul's Cathedral	Christopher Wren's building (1675–1710) replaced the medieval one, burned down in 1666
Westminster Abbey	Begun by Edward the Confessor in the 1040s
York Minster	England's biggest medieval cathedral with famous stained glass
Canterbury Cathedral	A church was first built on this site in 597; the present cathedral dates from the 1070s
Salisbury Cathedral	Tallest spire in England at 122 m

GLITTERING PALACES

A palace is the home of a king, queen or emperor, though some other buildings later came to be called palaces. In Italy in the 1400s, for example, every prince had a 'palazzo', or palace. The earliest palaces were built for the pharaohs of Egypt and the kings of Babylon and Crete. Palaces were centres of government as well as luxurious homes for the ruler. Some became cities in miniature, like the Imperial Palace within the Forbidden City in Beijing, China. Rulers have gone on building bigger and more splendid palaces, from Versailles outside Paris in the 1600s to today's palaces in Saudi Arabia and Brunei, built from oil revenues.

▲ *The Palace of Versailles in France was built for King Louis XIV in the 1600s. It took 40 years to complete, so rich and elegant were its decorations. Now a museum, the palace has 1,300 rooms, a famous Hall of Mirrors and its own private theatre.*

▲ *Russian emperors, or tsars, enjoyed the splendours of the Baroque-style Winter Palace (built 1754–62) in St Petersburg. It almost burned to the ground in 1837, but was rebuilt two years later and now houses the world-famous Hermitage Museum.*

▼ *The biggest palace ever built for a ruler was the Imperial Palace of the Chinese emperor. It stands within the walls of the Forbidden City, a walled area of China's capital city, Beijing. The only people allowed within the Forbidden City were the imperial family and their officials and servants. Inside the Imperial Palace, the emperor lived in solitary magnificence.*

▶▶	GREAT PALACES OF THE WORLD
Spain	Escorial and Alhambra in Granada; Alcazar in Seville
Italy	Doges' in Venice; Pitti in Florence
UK	Buckingham Palace and St James's in London; Holyrood in Scotland
France	Louvre in Paris; Versailles near Paris
Russia	Winter Palace in St Petersburg

▶ *During the 1400s the Italian city-state of Venice was at the height of its wealth and power, ruled by dukes, or 'doges'. These rulers lived in the Doges' Palace (shown here in the centre of the picture), a treasure-house of art. Next to the palace is Venice's most famous church, the Basilica of St Mark, and the tall bell tower, or Campanile.*

▲ *Not all palaces were homes for kings and queens. Blenheim Palace in England was built between 1705 and 1725 for the Duke of Marlborough, a famous soldier. The huge house was a thank-you from Queen Anne and her government for Marlborough's victories against the French. It became the family home of the Churchill family, and Winston Churchill, Britain's wartime prime minister, was born there in 1874.*

COLOSSAL CASTLES

Enormous amounts of time and effort went into building castles – defensive strongholds for rulers in times of war. Castle-building lasted for over 5,000 years, and was practised all around the world, from South America to New Zealand. Some of the biggest castles were built by Christian and Muslim soldiers during the Crusades, or Holy Wars, of the Middle Ages. The strongest medieval castles had stone walls up to 7 m thick, but cannons brought an end to castles as effective defences in the 1400s, and after that most castles were turned into houses or prisons.

▲ *The most spectacular Iron Age hill fort in Britain is Maiden Castle. Its earth walls and ditches, now grass-covered, presented a maze-like obstacle to any attacking army. Even so, the fort fell to Roman invaders in about AD 43, after a fierce battle.*

▲ *Neuschwanstein Castle in Bavaria, Germany, was never a home to knights, despite its appearance. The fantasy castle was in fact built in the steam-train age, in 1869, by mad King Ludwig II of Bavaria.*

▲ *Krak des Chevaliers in Syria is the biggest surviving Crusader castle. Rock walls dropped sheer on three sides, and the fourth side was protected by a moat. The Crusaders held this castle from 1142 until 1271, when they were tricked into surrendering to the Muslims.*

▼ *Many castles were built in India during the Mogul Empire (1500s to 1700s). The Red Fort in Delhi is surrounded by 30-m-high red sandstone walls, which enclose beautifully decorated pavilions and marble palaces decorated with gold and precious stones.*

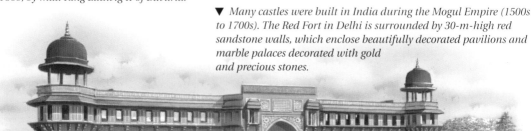

◄ *Chambord is a splendid example of a French 'chateau', a castle in name only. It was built as a large and luxurious home (it has 440 rooms) and not as a defensive stronghold, by the French kings Francis I and Henry I during the 1500s. By this time castles in France had lost their importance in war.*

►► **FIVE GREAT CASTLES**	
Hradcany	Prague, Czech Rep.
Krak des Chevaliers	Syria
Segovia	Spain
Beaumaris	Wales
Edinburgh	Scotland

▼ *Japanese castles of the 1500s and 1600s, such as Himeji, looked formidable, but had wooden walls filled in with clay and plaster. They were not built to withstand sieges or cannon-fire, since Japanese soldiers preferred fighting on open ground.*

KEEP OUT!
● Slit-like or cross-shaped openings in castle walls were used by archers, who could fire arrows through them without being seen by the enemy.
● In India, castle gateways had unusual defences – iron spikes in the doors to stop war elephants battering them open.
● A moat round a castle made it harder for invaders to reach the castle's walls.

▼ *Conwy Castle was built in north Wales from 1283 to 1287 by the English king, Edward I. It was one of a chain of castles built to help him conquer Wales. The eight strong, round towers were used for defence as well as for accommodation for the soldiers. Round towers had fewer blindspots than the traditional square 'keeps', or main towers.*

▲ *The fortress of Sacsayhuaman in Peru was built of enormous stones like these, some weighing over 100 tonnes, fitted together without cement. It was built by the Incas in 1520, but was pulled down by their Spanish conquerors.*

TREASURES LOST AND FOUND

In their search for gold and silver, treasure-hunters of fact and fiction have gone to extreme lengths. They have made dangerous journeys to far-off places, such as the mythical kingdom of El Dorado, or King Solomon's Mines. They have dug holes, dived into oceans and lakes, and pored over old maps to locate lost treasures – sunken ships, pirates' chests, and gold bars hidden by the Nazis during World War II. Most treasure, however, is found by archaeologists. Their discoveries include the tomb of the Egyptian boy-king Tutankhamun. But just occasionally, metal detectors also strike lucky!

▲ *This gold mask is often said to show Agamemnon, the Greek leader during the Trojan War, but it is probably older (about 1600 BC). It was found in a tomb in 1874 by German archaeologist Heinrich Schliemann.*

◀ *Among the finds in Tutankhamun's tomb was the gold death mask of the young king, found inside the burial chamber.*

▼ *The tomb of the boy-king Tutankhamun, who ruled Egypt from 1347 to 1339 BC, was discovered in Egypt's Valley of the Kings by British archaeologist Howard Carter in 1922. Unlike most Egyptian tombs, it was still mostly intact, though it had been robbed twice.*

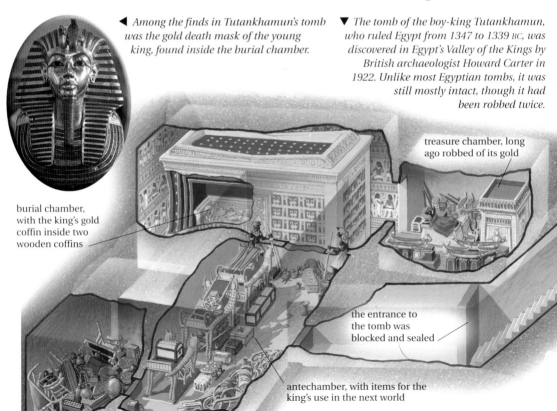

treasure chamber, long ago robbed of its gold

burial chamber, with the king's gold coffin inside two wooden coffins

the entrance to the tomb was blocked and sealed

antechamber, with items for the king's use in the next world

REMARKABLE ROMAN REMAINS	
9,213 Roman silver coins found on farmland in Somerset, southwest England	1998
11 Roman ships unearthed under a train station in Italy	1999
43 Roman gold coins found on a building site in London	2000

▼ *In 1939 a long-buried wooden ship was found at Sutton Hoo in eastern England. It was the grave of a great king, probably Redwald of East Anglia, who died about 627. The treasures included this iron helmet.*

◄ *When the Spanish Armada sailed to England in 1588, it carried gold as well as guns. Many Spanish ships were wrecked by storms as they tried to sail home, and ever since treasure-hunters have been searching for the lost Spanish gold.*

▶ *Precious stones such as diamonds, emeralds, rubies and sapphires have been treasured since ancient times. A single diamond can change hands for as much as £10 million, while the famous Kohinoor diamond is literally priceless!*

IT'S A FACT
In 1532 the Spanish conquistador Pizarro demanded a huge ransom to free the captured Inca leader Atahualpa. He wanted one room filled with gold, and another filled twice over with silver. The Incas paid up, but the Spaniards still killed the Inca leader. They then melted down many of the Inca treasures to make gold and silver bars.

◄ *The Mildenhall Treasure, a buried hoard of Roman silverware, was dug up in 1942 by a farmer ploughing his field in Suffolk in eastern England. Among the 34 pieces, now in the British Museum, London, was this large decorated dish, probably made in the AD 300s for a rich landowner.*

GREAT WALLS AND TOWERS

Walls are built to keep people in or out. The world's longest is the Great Wall of China, which extends for 6,400 km. One of the most mysterious walls is the 160-km-long earth bank known as the Eredo in Nigeria, Africa. This huge rampart, 22 m high in places and half-hidden by forest growth, is thought to be about 1,000 years old. Building it involved shifting more earth than was needed to build the Great Pyramid in Egypt. Walls often have watchtowers along their length, built as military lookouts or defensive positions. Other towers were built within medieval cities, many as lookouts, and some, particularly in Italy, as bell-towers beside churches.

▲ *The longest wall built by the Romans was Hadrian's Wall in northern Britain, which was built to control the frontier between Roman Britain and Scotland. It took the army eight years (AD 122–130) to complete. The turf and stone wall is 118 km long and has a 9-m-wide ditch on its northern side.*

▶ *The Leaning Tower of Pisa in Italy was built as a bell-tower. The 55-m high tower began to lean even before it was finished in the 1360s, because the ground was too soft to bear its weight. Modern engineers are trying to prevent it falling over, whilst allowing it to stay leaning, because people like it that way!*

◀ *The Eiffel Tower in Paris was the wonder of the age in the 1880s. Made of 6,000 tonnes of iron and steel, it stands 300 m high. When construction finished in 1889, the tower was the highest structure in the world.*

WORLD-FAMOUS WALLS

Great Wall of China	Averages 9 m high, with 12-m-high watchtowers every 60 m
Hadrian's Wall, England	Averages 6 m high, with milecastles, or forts, at intervals
Berlin Wall	Was 5 m high, 45 km long, with electrified fences and watchtowers

◀ *At 553 m high, the CN Tower (1976) in Toronto, Canada, is the world's highest tower – almost twice the height of the Eiffel Tower. Helicopters were used to lift the topmost sections into position.*

◀ *The most infamous wall of the 20th century was the Berlin Wall. Hastily erected by the East German Communists in 1961 to stop refugees fleeing to West Germany, the wall became a symbol of the Cold War. After Communism collapsed in East Germany in 1989, the wall was pulled down amid great rejoicing.*

▶ *The Great Wall of China is the longest structure ever built by humans. Completed in the 200s BC to defend China from northern invaders, the Great Wall winds for over 6,400 km, linking up stretches of old walls with new sections. Thousands of people died while building it, which is why it came to be called the longest cemetery in the world.*

MIGHTY MONUMENTS

Monuments are usually built to mark important events or famous people. The world's tallest monument is an arch, the Gateway to the West, in St Louis, USA, which commemorates the migration of thousands of people to the West in the 1800s. The Romans set up stone arches and columns as monuments. But the highest column in the world is more recent. It commemorates the battle of San Jacinto, fought between Texans and Mexicans in 1836. Another world-famous column is Nelson's Column in Trafalgar Square, London.

▲ *The Washington Monument in Washington, D.C., is the same shape as an Egyptian obelisk, but much bigger. Visitors can go up inside by lift, and descend by 898 steps!*

◄ *The Statue of Liberty is probably the most famous landmark in the USA. It measures 46 m from feet to torch, and stands on a 47-m-high, star-shaped pedestal, on an island at the entrance to New York Harbour. The statue was a gift to the United States from the people of France, and was opened in 1886 as a monument to American independence.*

◄ *Trajan's Column in Rome is a marble monument set up in AD 113 by Emperor Trajan, whose tomb is in the base. It stands 38 m high and is decorated with a detailed relief picture-strip showing the Roman army on campaign in Dacia (modern Romania).*

⟩⟩ FIVE MIGHTY MONUMENTS

	MONUMENT	PLACE	HEIGHT
★1	Gateway to the West	St Louis, USA	192 m
2	San Jacinto Monument	Texas, USA	173 m
3	Washington Monument	Washington, D.C.	169 m
4	Motherland Calls statue	Volgograd, Russia	82 m
5	The Monument	London, UK	61 m

a tram takes visitors to an observation room at the top

stainless steel plates reflect the sun

▲ The biggest stone heads in the world loom out from Mount Rushmore in South Dakota, USA. Each head is as big as a five-storey building! The Mount Rushmore National Memorial honours four US Presidents: Washington, Jefferson, Theodore Roosevelt and Lincoln.

◀ Russia's most famous tsar, Peter the Great, is commemorated by a huge statue of himself on horseback in St Petersburg. The entire city is a monument to Peter, who founded it in 1703 as a 'window to the West'.

◀ The Gateway to the West is the world's tallest steel monument. Completed in 1965, this 192-m-high arch honours the pioneers who set out from St Louis, Missouri, to settle in the American West after 1803. The arch is as wide as it is high.

two theatres and a museum are at the base of the arch

GODS AND GODDESSES

Christians, Muslims and Jews believe that there is only one God, a supreme creator of all things. In other religions, especially ancient religions, many gods and goddesses appear. Some of these supernatural beings were thought to live in nature – in rivers, trees or rocks. Others were linked to animals, such as buffaloes, elephants or eagles. In ancient Mesopotamia, there were gods of the sky, water and wind. In Egypt and Central America, the chief god was the Sun-god, while in ancient Greece an entire family of gods was thought to live on top of Mount Olympus. Some of them were helpful to humans, others could be mischievous or violent.

KEY TO THE GREEK GODS

1	Zeus
2	Hera
3	Hermes
4	Poseidon
5	Pan
6	Athena
7	Aphrodite
8	Ares
9	Artemis
10	Hades

▲ *Chief of the Greek gods and goddesses was Zeus, king of the gods, who might hurl a thunderbolt from the skies to show his displeasure. Zeus's brother, Hades, was god of the Underworld and the dead, and Zeus's messenger was the winged Hermes. The Romans adopted these gods, but gave them new names. Zeus, for example, became known as Jupiter.*

▲ *The story of how God saved Noah from the Flood, which was God's punishment for people's wickedness, is told in the Old Testament of the Bible. Noah built a great ark, and with his family and two of all God's animals, he waited for the Flood to go down.*

▶ *In Christianity, dragons often represent evil, for example in the many pictures of St George killing a dragon. But in China the dragon is a godlike creature with power to do good. The dragon became China's national symbol, and huge paper dragons are paraded in New Year celebrations. In Taoist belief the dragon symbolises the power of nature.*

Chinese New Year paper dragon supported on sticks

◀ *One of the most popular Hindu gods is Hanuman, the monkey-god (shown here as a gold figure). In the long story called the Ramayana, Hanuman helps to rescue Prince Rama's wife from a demon. Monkeys (left) in India are treated with reverence by Hindus, in honour of Hanuman.*

▶ *The Egyptian Sun-god was Ra, creator of the world and lord of the sky. Egypt's kings called themselves 'sons of Ra', and the god took many forms, including a bird, a snake, and a man with a ram's head.*

	TOP GREEK GODS
Zeus	King of the gods
Poseidon	God of the sea
Athena	Goddess of wisdom and war
Apollo	God of music and prophecy
Hades	God of the Underworld

MYTHS AND LEGENDS

Myths and legends are stories that have been told for hundreds of years – stories of gods and goddesses, heroes and monsters with unusual powers, and perilous quests in search of a person, object or truth. Ancient stories in many cultures tell how the world was formed, or explain why the Sun rises and sets each day, or tell of mythical animals that may be friendly or fearsome. No one knows how much truth lies behind such stories, or whether they are based on history or the imagination!

▶ *The Minotaur was a terrifying monster with a bull's head on a human body. It lived in the Labyrinth, a maze of underground tunnels, on the island of Crete, and fed on human victims brought to it as sacrifices. It was finally killed by the hero Theseus.*

▼ *Centaurs were mythological creatures, said by Greek story-tellers to be half-human and half-horse. Most centaurs were wild and dangerous, but the centaur Chiron was wise and taught the Greek hero Achilles how to play music and how to hunt.*

▶▶ MYTHICAL SUPER-HEROES	
Sigurd, dragon slayer	German/Norse
Cuchulainn	Celtic
Hercules	Greek/Roman

▼ *The phoenix was a remarkable magical bird. There was just one, in Arabia, and it lived for 500 years before making a funeral nest that burst into flames. From the cooling ashes, another phoenix emerged. The story may originally have come from Egypt.*

▶▶ MENACING MONSTERS	
The Minotaur	Half-man, half-bull, killed in Labyrinth by Theseus
The Hydra	A many-headed snake, slain by Hercules
Medusa	One of three Gorgons; could turn people to stone

»	GREEK SUPER-HEROES	
Hercules	Performed 12 astonishing feats of strength and bravery, such as killing lions with his bare hands	
Bellerophon	Rode the winged horse Pegasus and slew Chimaera, a monster with lion's head/goat's body	
Jason	Led the Argonauts in search of the Golden Fleece	
Perseus	Slew Medusa; used his shield as a mirror so her gaze turned herself to stone, and not him	

◄ *Mermaids were said to sing songs that lured men to them so they could entice them beneath the waves, where they drowned. The legend of the mermaid may be based on sailors' glimpses of sea mammals such as dugongs or seals, which can look half-human in the water.*

► *St George, England's patron saint, was a legendary hero of Asia Minor (Turkey) in the* AD *200s. The story was told that George killed a terrible dragon and saved the local people, who became Christians. Crusaders returning to England in the 1200s brought the story back with them.*

▲ *The horn of a unicorn was said to have magical medicinal powers. But only a pure maiden could capture the shy, dangerous creature.*

▼ *According to legend, Rome was founded by twins named Romulus and Remus. Cast adrift on the River Tiber as babies, they were found and suckled by a wolf. In 753* BC*, the brothers founded Rome, but later they quarrelled and Remus was killed.*

► *King Arthur is the best and noblest of all the British legendary heroes, a mixture of possible fact and fantastic fiction. Here the young king is shown drawing the magical sword Excalibur from the stone, a feat that only he was able to do – thus proving himself the rightful king of Britain.*

MONSTERS AND SUPERSTITIONS

People are often ready to believe in the unbelievable – mysterious animals, monsters, vampires, werewolves, witches, ghouls and even aliens from space. The truth is we like being scared by spooky stories that cannot be explained! In Scotland, 'Nessie' the Loch Ness Monster, once believed to be a giant reptilian relic from prehistoric times, has evaded all attempts to film or catch it in the murky lake. The world's most famous hairy 'ape-men', the Yeti of the Himalayas and Bigfoot of the North American forests, are also shy of the camera. Could these elusive creatures be real?

▲ *In 1967 amateur film of a hairy, humanlike creature in the forests of California aroused great excitement. The film, along with photos and footprints, has been used as proof of North America's own Yeti, known as Sasquatch, or Bigfoot, although scientists have not yet been convinced.*

▼ *Witches were said to take on animal shapes. This may be the origin of the werewolf legend, in which a person transforms into a wolf and becomes a savage monster, seeking out human victims. In Africa, people were said to turn into leopards.*

THE YETI

● Nicknamed the Abominable Snowman by climbers, the Yeti is said to roam the snowy Himalayas of Asia. Photos of 'Yeti footprints' were taken in 1951, but scraps of skin and droppings have not yet provided enough evidence to prove that this remarkable creature truly exists.

» COMMON SUPERSTITIONS	
Black cats	Lucky or unlucky!
Spilling salt	Unlucky. To undo the bad luck, throw salt over your left shoulder
Friday	The unluckiest day of the week
Breaking a mirror	Seven years' bad luck
Number 13	Unlucky
Number 7	Lucky

◀ *The blood-sucking vampire of the screen has nothing to do with the vampire bat of South America. The original Dracula was a medieval tyrant named Vlad the Impaler, who stuck his victims on stakes. Comic books and films created all kinds of variations on the vampire theme.*

▶ *Legends abound of giant snakes. One called the Grootslang is said to lurk in a deep cavern in South Africa, guarding a hoard of diamonds. People often exaggerate the size of the snake they have seen out of fear.*

SPOOKY BELIEFS	
Ghosts	Borley Rectory, England's most haunted house (1863, burned down 1939)
Kraken	Biggest of all sea monsters (as big as an island); found in the sea off Norway
Witches	Salem, Massachusetts, largest witch-hunt in American history (1692);
	19 men and women were hanged as witches
Vampires	Fictional pointy-toothed, deathly pale creatures from Transylvania, Romania
Werewolves	Called *loupgarou* in France, where they reputedly dig up corpses

▶ *Cats have been both worshipped and feared by people throughout history. Witches' cats were thought to be demons in disguise. In medieval France, black cats were roasted to make cures for evil spells! But in Britain black cats are generally regarded as lucky.*

▲ *Reports of mysterious Unidentified Flying Objects, or UFOs, including fiery chariots and floating dishes, crop up through history. The 'flying saucer' became front-page news in the 1950s, with a flurry of sightings and photos of alleged visitors from outer space – most of them clearly fakes.*

« 6. Egypt » 7. Cambodia » 8. Pakistan » 9. St Peter's Basilica » 10. King Louis XIV » 11. A bell-tower » 17. The Minotaur » 18. St Louis » 19. Turkey » 20. Unidentified Flying Object

WONDERS OF THE WORLD *QUIZ*

Now that you have read all about the biggest and best Wonders of the World, see if you can answer these 20 quiz questions! (Pictures give clues, answers at the top of the page.)

▶ *3. In which country is Ayers Rock?*

▲ *1. Name the world's biggest canyon.*

◀ *2. Who built the Taj Mahal in India?*

▼ *4. How tall is the tallest pyramid?*

▲ *5. How many ancient wonders of the world were there?*

▶ *6. The Lighthouse at Alexandria was built in which country?*

▼ *7. In which country is the temple-city of Angkor Wat?*

▼ *8. Which country has the biggest mosque?*

▶ *9. What is the name of the biggest church in Europe?*

▶ *10. The Palace of Versailles was built for which French king?*

» 1.The Grand Canyon » 2. Shah Jahan, The Mogul Emperor of India » 3. Australia » 4. It is 148 m tall » 5. Seven » 12. Tutankhamun » 13. In 1889 » 14. Washington, D.C. » 15. The Great Wall of China » 16. Zeus

▼ 12. This gold death mask belonged to which Egyptian king?

◀ 13. In what year was the Eiffel Tower completed?

▲ 14. The Washington Monument is found in which US city?

▲ 11. The Leaning Tower of Pisa was originally built as what?

▼ 15. What is the largest structure ever built?

▲ 16. Who was king of the ancient Greek gods?

▲ 17. What is the name of this mythical monster?

▼ 20. What do the letters UFO stand for?

▶ 18. In which American city can you find the Gateway to the West?

▲ 19. The legend of St George comes originally from which modern country?

INDEX

The publishers wish to thank the following artists who have contributed to this book:
Julie Banyard, Jim Channell, Terry Gabbey, Peter Gregory, Alan Hancocks, Richard Hook, John James, Andy Lloyd-Jones, Kevin Maddison, Martin Sanders, Rob Sheffield, Roger Smith, Mike Taylor (SGA), Rudi Vizi

The publishers wish to thank the following sources for the photographs used in this book:
CORBIS: Page 15 (T/L) Cordaiy Photo Library Ltd; Page 15 (C) Layne Kennedy; Page 29 (B/L) Brian Vikander
All other photographs from Miles Kelly Archives